WIMBLEDON SCHOOL OF ART

MERTON HALL ROAD · SW19 3QA

Telephone: 020 8408 5000

Dilys Jackson

Sculptor

This volume is published on the occasion of the exhibition
Dilys Jackson: Watercourse
March 2003

Designed by Dianne Setch
Printed by Zenith Media, Cardiff

ISBN   0-9544439-0-X
Published by Dilys Jackson, 22 Llanbleddian Gardens, Cardiff, CF24 4AT, Wales, UK

cover	REMWAS (Ready Made War Scenarios) 1989
opposite	Portrait with Jackdaw 1994

Contents

Foreword

I first met Dilys Jackson when she was working with autistic children in the Lindens School in Penarth. I was a councillor at the time and was visiting the school in that role. Since then, for over 20 years, I have had a valued friendship with Dilys, sometimes seeing her very frequently, preparing for events like International Women's Day and the Women's Arts Festival (this aimed to give every woman who wanted, the opportunity to display a work of art and take part in promoting women in the arts). Dilys was one of the core group of women who worked with the Women's Committee of South Glamorgan County Council to develop opportunities for women in the arts.

Over the years I have seen Dilys' strong vibrant work shown in many places. I have a postcard on my desk of one of her paintings. It was exhibited in the Women's Arts Festival. When I think of Dilys I think of strength and determination and of strong, rugged landscapes. I had the privilege of opening Dilys' exhibition at St David's Hall, Cardiff in 1995.

I am proud to write this foreword. I have enjoyed my friendship with Dilys. We have both been part of a wider group of women who enjoyed the arts, had a lot of fun and used every initiative possible to overcome bureaucracy and make the arts a living entity in Cardiff. What I learned has helped in my role as an MP. Dilys' contribution to women, the arts and to politics in Cardiff has been immense.

Julie Morgan MP

Dilys Jackson in her Cardiff studio 1991

10

figure 1   Life Painting 1959

Introduction

The Slade School of Fine Art has always held a prestigious position among art schools and has seen many of Britain's recognised artists evolve from the raw enthusiast to the virtuoso. It was in the 1950s when post war insecurity was receding, when London was celebrating notable, international art exhibitions again, that Dilys Jackson embarked on her journey to become an artist. She entered the Slade to begin the studies that would lead her to the strengths of her artistic performance.

The Slade's reputation centred on the art of the life room. Painting students were encouraged to paint and draw from the model and as the teachers worked strongly within the historical spirit of the school, it was a very determined and brave student who moved away from the life room. I moved my painting activity to the largest landing on the main staircase, gaining space for work unrelated to the easel and more influenced by the American abstract expressionists. Dilys descended into the dusty basement to engage with the mysterious practice of three dimensional representation. Sculpture at that time was very much a male domain dominated by physical power so I believed it was an extraordinarily courageous move.

There has, I presume, always been a competitive argument between painters and sculptors but in the late 1950s it rose as a very heated debate in many quarters. The quip much repeated at that time, attributed to an American painter 'Sculpture is what you fall over when you stand back to look at a painting' didn't invade my perceptions, possibly because when I stood back on the landing to look at my paintings I fell down the stairs. When I entered the hallowed spaces of the Mayfair galleries I took in and enjoyed all the art around. This was a period when the Rock 'n Roll of painting hit London with exhibitions of large scale work by American abstract artists but it was also a time when the quieter insistence of modern European sculpture was exposed.

Students were influenced by the changes taking place in the making of art and the debate about abstraction gradually brought the academies into the mainstream of the development of contemporary art in Britain. It was an exciting time to be launching one's career as an artist.

Dilys, from the centre of this time, embarked on her singular path as a sculptor. The necessities of making an income, raising a family and running a home take their toll on the time and brain space of many artists, particularly women, but throughout the years when a personal art practice took second place to growing children, Dilys increased her drive and maintained a credible artistic production.

12 The legacy of her bravery in going down the stairs to the sculpture basement at the Slade is evident in her travels. Pacing alone around the base of Ayers Rock is to make a drawing of that giant sculpture with a three dimensional, sensory pencil. There is no respite, no holiday for the artist.

Throughout the years threads of form and subject have evolved, crystallised and matured in Dilys' sculpture and drawings. Her concerns about equality, the desolation wrought by war and the often unsung and non-recognised role of women in art and in society hover around her sculptures. The juxtaposition of materials, the images culled from the environment of her expeditions and the use of personal, visual experiences are statements about her big, world observations.

'Retirement age' sees Dilys at her most prolific. I know her production will go on and on as she rejoices in the making of art. I am so pleased that my time in the melting pot of ideas coincided with when Dilys set out on her journey too, otherwise we may never have met and enjoyed a special friendship. Life would have been the poorer.

Terry Setch RWA

13

figure 2   Wendover in the Snow 1960

Making Opposites Meet
Dilys Jackson, sculptor and environmental artist

To use the term 'environmental artist' is likely to suggest that Dilys Jackson is someone who works closely with the natural world and who may make sculptures that are created as an essential part of the site on which they are to be seen. There is certainly a sense in which this could describe her way of working, both as an artist engaged with public spaces and because of her personal responses to landscape. However, the term is also capable of stretching to fit a much wider concern with both the environment in which we live and also the circumstances that affect the balance and equality of nature and society. Dilys Jackson's career embraces all these with a passion and commitment which began at the age of seven when she 'decided she was going to be an artist'. We talked about her life and her work in the context of various decades, but of course, things don't fit that neatly and anyway ideas and ideals that emerge at one period of one's life tend to develop and nudge at each other in others. In fact, one of the first points that Dilys makes about her work is that there are series on a particular theme or approach and yet there are also clear links between these series. In spending time talking, looking through drawers of large drawings, handling small bronze sculptures and levering our way through the stacks of larger paintings and collages, we were constantly spinning out the strands that have made these links so important.

figure 3   Indian Pitta 1945

figure 4   Puppy 1955

Dilys Jackson lives in the centre of Cardiff and commutes to Tondu in the Llynfi Valley and to Port Talbot, where she works as an artist for a Groundwork Trust (Groundwork Bridgend and Neath Port Talbot). Her connections with Wales are a part of the complicated strands of her life story. She had Scottish, English and Welsh grandparents of whom the latter lived in the Abergavenny area, although this must have seemed remote to a girl born in Sri Lanka and who spent her early girlhood in South Africa. She did her Art Teacher Training in Swansea and later

lived, with her husband and sons, in Penarth, where she taught autistic children for many years. At the end of the 1980s she studied for an MA at University of Wales Institute Cardiff and since 1994 she has worked as a facilitator for community art projects associated with the physical regeneration of the post industrial urban environment of the South Wales valleys. In many respects her art education and development as an artist were typical of the post-War generation who had a more or less traditional introduction to the formal skills of drawing, painting and sculpture, but who were about to see huge changes in the theory and practice of art. However, she recalls her very first introduction to drawing as being more unusual. While still living in Sri Lanka, she was

figure 5   Owl 1972

taught to draw according to the instructions that came as part of a syllabus devised for parents teaching their children at home. She continued to take art seriously while at secondary school in Cambridge, studying extra classes in ceramics and print making at Homerton College and life drawing at the local art college. She recalls working with a friend to make an eight foot long lino print. The small clay figures made at this time are tentative experiments in handling three dimensional form, but suggest that she was already developing skills in observation from life and in the simplification of form.

figure 6   Lost Scrolls 1972

16

Dilys won a place at the Slade School of Art in 1956 and chose sculpture as her subsidiary subject. Her skills in clay modelling and carving developed and they still form the basis of her three dimensional work. At the Slade she met her husband whose career initially affected her own. It took them first to Essex and then to Spain. Dilys explained, with a touch of amusement, that she and their two sons were supported by money from the Welsh Church Fund "...for the dependents of poor scholars". Later they made the move to Wales and Dilys's own career as a teacher began. For a number of years her practice as a sculptor were reduced and the next significant steps in this respect came in the early 1970s. The development of her work in wood and stone at this time illustrates a love of clear, strong form and of contrasts in shape affected by light and shadow on surfaces. Here too the influence of the founders of early modern sculpture appears to have come to the surface.

Works such as the wooden *Torso* 1974 pay some tribute to the simplifying force of Barbara Hepworth's sculpture, while the resin *Head* and the stone carved *Owl* dip into the wide pool of Henry Moore's impact on British Post War sculpture.

Events external to the world of art were also to exert a great influence on the development of Dilys Jackson's work. Other than links with other artists and involvement with trends in art, she marks her progress by reference to political issues and to moral situations. Her politicisation began in the late 1950s, while living in London. The Campaign for Nuclear Disarmament began and it engaged many of her generation. She recalls attending the CND meeting at Westminster Hall when Bertrand Russell addressed the protesters and then going to voice the protest outside 10 Downing Street. Later the Cuban crisis increased her sense of world threat and of impending political catastrophe but it was the protests at Greenham Common during the 1980s that really stimulated her politically and also proved to have had an important effect on her work as an artist. Dilys Jackson was already making work on the theme of barriers, victims and death. The United States and British soldiers maintained and guarded the Cruise nuclear missiles inside the sealed perimeter fence but missiles were also regularly and furtively taken under heavy escort to other bases in Britain. Protest focused on peaceful circling of the fence at Greenham, the display of banners and occasional risky sorties to cross over the barriers. Dilys joined the protest. She took away with her from her visits to Greenham a compulsion in her artwork to make statements against war and its consequences. This theme and the moral necessity driving it have persisted in the work from the last two decades.

We are all aware of the way in which a high fence or gate imposes itself on our sense of space and even of freedom. We have looked cautiously and sometimes admiringly at magnificent decorative iron gates and huge walls that symbolise prosperity, privacy and power. However, such things also symbolise privilege, restraint and exclusion. In a world where barriers are increasingly associated with a dangerous, aggressive and prohibitive society there is none so intimidating and frightening as those erected to collude in genocide and torture.

18

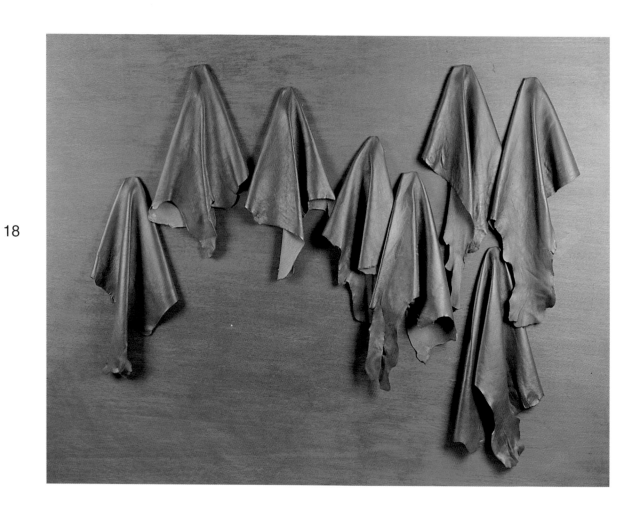

figure 7   Dark Hanging Group 1974

Dilys Jackson's barrier images are not specific, they always consist of close upright forms, jagged at their edges, tightly bound with thongs and apparently isolated in space. They are multiplied by her use of different media, drawings in pastel and charcoal, collages with paper, wood, leather and wool. The images of barriers are partnered by those of victims. These are not the realistically horrific shots to which we are familiarised by journalism, but sinister packaged bodies, shrouded in their 'body-bags'. They tend to resemble the barriers, but this time they are folded and lying prone, helpless and depleted. Some are victims of torture, such as the Kuwaiti people taken by Iraq, others the destitute South American street children lying wrapped in their paper sheets. Although the 'Gulf War' of 1990 provided the immediate impulse for much of the latter work, this had a wider significance as a reflection on the personal consequences of wars, even those fought at a distance with long-range weapons. Dilys goes through her large drawings and turns to the theme of the city and civilization itself as the victim. She holds up images of *Burning Cities* depicted as sharp, shattered architectural forms set against flaming colours. There are relief drawings of destruction made with debris of tattered strips of wood or dried rush leaves.

By the end of the 1980s Dilys had decided to study for the M.A. at Cardiff Institute. Her work during 1987-89 compressed the theme of atrocity, war and protest into a coherent body of work. The starting point was Greenham and images of watchtowers that transmuted themselves into birds of prey. Several of the series of drawings in charcoal and wash depict the harsh planked shape of a tower standing on four supports against a stormy sky and the rough land found on common ground. Others depict ragged black shapes, the planking torn into huge wings and the supporting structure becoming stilt-like legs. The 'birds of prey' lean forward, filling the picture space with menace. These are among her most dramatic works, belonging to a bizarre theatre of atrocity. By contrast, the majority of her images are still, solemn and portentous and as the M.A. study progressed the work tended towards images that are memorials – silent, vertical presences made from plaster and wood or pieces referring to the tattered flags and banners that remind us of battle and death. This phase of her work culminated in a large installation,

20

figure 8   Threatening Bird 1987

figure 9   Bodycase 1 1990
figure 10   Bodycase 2 1990

figure 11   Standing Stones 1988

known as *REMWAS (Readymade War Scenarios)*, made of elements that resemble packing cases. The dark coffin-like shapes filled a room and imposed a feeling of oppression onto the space. She explained that the reference to packing cases was associated with the idea of "…a production line of victims". Her victims were mute types, not individuals, but they encompassed the spectrum of suffering experienced as a result of war, such as the *Mourning Woman*, the *Raped Woman* and the *Dying Soldier*. Each of these six different 'figures' was repeated nine times, so that they fill an area of about sixty by fifteen feet. Some lie prone, end-to-end, others stand upright or lean forward in the familiar pose of an infantry soldier carrying a fixed bayonet or gun. Each type of 'victim' was based on a specific image that the artist had seen in a media photograph or as figures depicted on war memorials. The *Dead Child* came from a photograph of a father carrying the limp corpse of his young child and *Mourning Woman* from that of a Middle Eastern woman, whose hands were raised in expression of her grief. In the same year she made *Big Coat*, an installation for the Cardiff Visual Arts Festival, which was also another comment on war. The huge coat was strung over a wire frame, revealing its empty interior, as if waiting for some giant to shrug it on. Its purpose was to remind us that in putting on uniforms people take on roles and that those roles may come with duties that involve a blind acceptance of violence towards others.

The 1980s was a period of significant personal development for Dilys Jackson, for which her M.A. provided a focal point. However, her interest in women's issues had also been with her since her involvement with the Greenham protest, mainly staged by women. The interest was freshly kindled by studying Art History as a part of the M.A. course, for which she wrote a seminar paper titled "Men don't wear skirts". The experience of seeing Judy Chicago's *Dinner Party* many years previously, an amazing collaborative work which celebrated women's achievements throughout history, also stimulated a sense of rage at the knowledge that so many female achievements had been suppressed. Dilys joined the 'Women's Art Discussion Group', which was an offshoot of the 'Women's Committee of South Glamorgan'. They discussed the needs of women as artists in South Wales and out of these discussions came the idea of a 'Women's Art Festival'

figure 12   Derelict War Memorial 1986

24

figure 13   Victim Kuwait 1990

25

figure 14   Burning Cities 1989

to address the feelings of isolation that so many of them suffered. The Festival and the Womens' Arts Association,'Permanent Waves', have been an important support to Dilys Jackson and other women artists for about fifteen years.

The phrase "making opposites meet" first came to mind in relation to Dilys Jackson's work when we were talking about her interest in landscape and how that has translated into a body of artwork, which is ongoing. It was this aspect of her work that initially drew my attention to her and with which I feel most affinity. Places are important to her, very different places, such as the Canadian Rockies, the Omani Desert, Monument Valley in Arizona, Ayers Rock in Australia and the Ogwr and Garw valleys. Her experience of landscape is a sensuous one and it leads to an emphasis on the way that land is formed and changed. She also relates it to her own body and she particularly describes the South Wales valley forms as corporal in their undulations and curves. As a result both drawings and sculpture dealing with the landscape theme are characterised by strong formal shapes and contrasts between flowing, soft forms and harder shapes that often enclose a more gentle element.

In 1990 she started making a series of sculptures in bronze or stone in which she explores very simple forms. She refers to these as being like doughnuts, which have one surface that presents itself in a three dimensional way. In talking about these sculptures Dilys Jackson refers to the influence that early modernist artists, such as Barbara Hepworth, Ben Nicholson and Kandinsky had on the idea that the basic formality of shape can appeal and even move one through its purely physical form. She wanted to exploit this idea in her own way. The initial sculptures resulted from a master class in bronze casting that she took with Martin Bellwood in 1990. She made sledges out of wood and metal, of the kind that plasterers use to make architectural covings, and she established three basic shapes. These were the 'doughnut' with a wide hole, a closed 'doughnut' and a cylinder. She took numerous wax casts from these moulds and began to cut them, to re-set the planes and to fit them together. One of the strongest of this series is *Balance I*, the sculpture in which the perfect 'doughnut' is penetrated by the bent cylindrical shape. This seems to

figure 15   Balance I 1991

figure 16   Opposing Forms 1990

figure 17   Bronze 5 1991

represent the archetypal idea of masculine and feminine elements. The whole series also relates to Dilys Jackson's awareness that it is through the way that the parts of our bodies are made and fit together that we have a sense of our body and its movements and the outside world. When she went to work for a while in the Portland quarries in Dorset and was using soft sandstone she began to make sculptures combining pieces of stone with her bronze shapes. As well as extending her exploration of contrasting forms, this juxtaposition also exaggerated the apparent softness of the curved elements in *Balance* so that they seem as if they are sinking into a stone cushion.

More recently, since 2001 she has been making small sculptures that she sometimes calls 'toys' as they are intended to be held, to be piled up, to be played with. These developed into the *Seed* or *Pod* group and there is often a resemblance to an organic form. They also relate to certain forms found in landscapes, such as huge boulders that have been rolled into shape by glacial ice or split through by running water or by an interior event within the stone. However, the sculptures are also intended to suggest gender opposites through contrasts of indentation and bulging as the shape is explored through turning the sculpture in one's hands. Some of this series combine bronze and clay. The result of using fired clay is satisfying, producing mysterious, distorted ovoid shapes and smoky, sensuous surfaces.

A Leighton Studios Residency at Banff Center for the Arts, Canada, in 1994, enabled Dilys Jackson's practice to develop as a result of experimental work produced there. She had the opportunity to work with raku fired ceramics and also slumped glass, taking her moulds from pieces of bark. The huge mountains also stimulated her to imitate their character with folded, crumpled sheets of clay, wax and bronze. Dilys Jackson reworked her 'doughnut' forms, now penetrating the polished golden bronze form with oxidised elements that were cast from bark. The reference to landscape developed still mindful of the links to body parts, of which we are reminded in our everyday reference to parts of a landscape by words that describe the body, neck, shoulder, breast, arm, and nipple. In lingering over these

figure 18   Arch Formation 1995

32

figure 19   Flow from Arch 1996

figure 20   Bronze 1 1991

sculptures we discussed the way in which we often relate the way that we feel about a landscape to our own body sensations and that humans tend to respond to mountains especially as being symbolic of a fundamental physical experience or need. They certainly suggest power and are frequently associated with an uplifting spiritual awareness. However, there is also a sense in which the apparent structure of a particular landscape reveals the otherwise hidden secrets of its age and how it has been formed. The Canadian Rocky Mountains are tall and very rugged because they are new within the geological timescale. Dilys Jackson began to make sculptures that reflect the anatomy of that landscape, using more pointed shapes, harshly cleft with thin sheets of silver plated bronze or by turbulent, twisting outpourings of roughened metal. Some of the small pod or seed sculptures, such as *Blown Moss* (1998), burst into a type of growth as shoots of leaf-like bronze push through their sides and their apexes.

The visit to Canada came just before beginning her work with the Groundwork Trust in Glamorgan late in 1994 and so some of the ideas were transferred to her observation of the Welsh valleys. Dilys Jackson's work relating to the Ogwr and Garw valleys, and that inspired by her visit to Ayers Rock, are similar in the way that a flood of water is squeezed between bold compressing land forms. Her visit to Uluru, Ayers Rock, the famous Australian World Heritage site, was inspiring and she was lucky to be at the site when it rained and to see the way in which rain water cascading down the surface of the huge, red sandstone outcrop caused the streaks of blue and silver colour to form on the surface. While the Ayers Rock pastel drawings glow with the strange colour of the red stone, the Welsh drawings have darker, moodier colours, befitting the subtle light and variable weather that we experience. The only drawings that emphasise the straight and flat, the inexorable distances of a desert landscape are those made of a man-made watercourse in the Middle East. Anyone who visits Dilys Jackson's studio or sees an exhibition of her work will notice that she is equally committed to making drawings and sculptures. Drawing is important in that it gets ideas down fast. However, she doesn't see the relationship between the two media as simply that between preparatory and final work. She explains, "...drawing and sculpture are so different as symbolic systems.

figure 21   Sulphur Mountain 1994

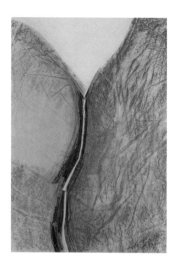  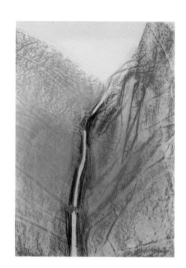

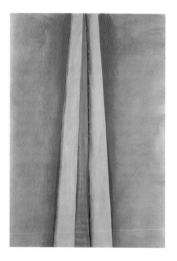  

figure 22
Cascade by Sunlit Rock 1994
figure 25
Channel Wadi Khatwa 1992

figure 23
Broken Cascade 1994
figure 26
Huntsman's Leap I 1995

figure 24
Broken Cascade III 1994
figure 27
Huntsman's Leap II 1995

figure 28   Pod 2000

Sculpture exists in three dimensions and therefore there is no question of its right to be." She points out that a painting or a drawing has to have some descriptive symbols or clues, which point the way towards what is observed in the real world. However, sculpture can forgo this necessity and so she says "...sculptures stand for themselves and don't explain." Many of her recent sculptures have a similar character to the drawings mentioned above. However she has also developed a transitional format through making three dimensional relief drawings, which will be made into sheet metal versions. She continues to make other sculptures in bronze and they exploit the various ways in which the material can be used, contrasting the polished arched or triangular shapes representing the land with the textured, irregular spills of roughened bronze that describe water.

Dilys Jackson's own practice as an artist runs parallel with her work as a community artist and facilitator and clearly, since 1994, much of her energy and time has been occupied in working with groups of people in the Bridgend and Neath Port Talbot areas to enable them to make works of art that will improve the environment in which they live. However, she sometimes also undertakes other residencies or commissions or takes part in outdoor sculptural events. On several occasions the Festival at Lower Machen near Caerffili gave sculptors an opportunity to exhibit work in the vicinity of the church. Dilys Jackson accepted an invitation to take part in 1989. She chose to make a piece of work especially for this site and decided to use the relic base of an ancient 'preaching cross' as the starting point for her work. Proclamation, the pyramidal slab that covered the base and, in a sense, replaced the original cross, was made with a mirror surface that visually reflected the sky or heavens down onto earth and also reached upwards in a symbol of aspiration. In 1997 she took part in the Coed Hills Rural Artspace project, Y Adwy, during which artists make temporary installations amongst the woodlands and fields. Secret was a discrete piece made from beech twigs and branches forming a kind of screen or enclosure, while Message was the most extensive work in the project, forming a link of larch poles aligned with an oak tree at Coed Hills and the two mile distant St Hilary television mast.

figure 29   Message 1997

figure 30
Ceramic and Bronze 1994
figure 33
Pod Growth 2001

figure 31
Moss Bell 1998
figure 34
Fire 1999

Figure 32
Granny Bronze 1998
figure 35
Blown Moss 1998

figure 36   Quarry and Culvet 1997
figure 37   Long Stream 1996

There have been opportunities to make more permanent statements relating to particular sites and to spaces used by people. One of the most significant happened in 1993-95 when she was asked to make the *Sight Garden* for Stackpole Centre in Pembrokeshire, where many disabled people stay on courses and holidays. The intention of the garden was to enable people with sight to appreciate that faculty and to lead them to enjoy and think about visual illusion. All the various elements in the sculpture and of the planting were connected to the eye and the artist also employed the mathematical principles of the Fibonacci series as the basis for spacing and proportion. The central five metre diameter 'pool' of stainless steel represented the pupil of the eye and the graded slate surround its iris. From the central feature ringed with reclaimed bricks, one looks out towards a circle of trees that is marked by the fine line of a single course of bricks and beyond to a path that is like a tongue leading the eye to a mirror, while the illusion of an archway with a pathway behind opens up the outer brick wall of the garden. Dilys Jackson's commission at the Greenfield Country Park in Clwyd was part of a project to create sculptures that were responses to, and interpretations of the industrial history of the site. Her copper-red brick sculpture occupies a ground space about fifteen feet long on which blue fired bricks repeat the pattern of the shapes of the five pools created for industrial use that are in the Greenfield Valley. The brick 'platform' rolls out like the rolls of embossed copper that were once made in the mill. Local people worked with the artist to carve the individual blue toned bricks with images relating to river life and with the names of the five pools.

It is salutary to meet an artist like Dilys Jackson, who is so committed to working with people and to the natural and the built environment. However, it is doubly satisfying to find that her studio work also pursues ideas and approaches that are intellectual and humanitarian. There is a completeness to this type of practice of art and to the person who makes it. However, through all our discussions about her work and her interests there remains with me the depth of her feelings about the wastefulness of war. It is a theme that perhaps also quietly informs her love of the landscape and of people because conflict and greed can damage both irreparably.

Shelagh Hourahane 2002

43

figure 38   Rain Pool 1993-5

44

figure 39   Waterworn 2001

figure 40   Waterfall 2000

46

figure 41
Gorse 2000
figure 43
Forest Edge 2000

figure 42
Head of the Valley, Spring 2000
figure 44
Dark Valley 2000

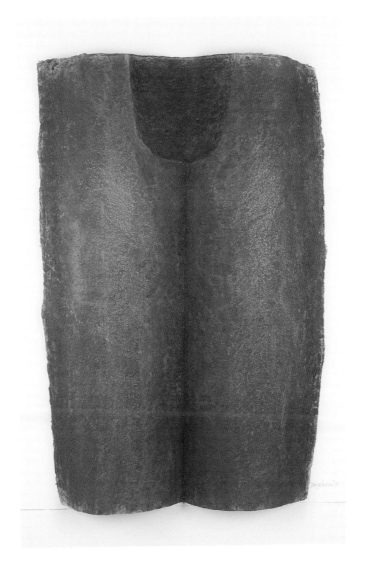

47

figure 45   Rust 1999

48

figure 46   Garw Quarry 2002

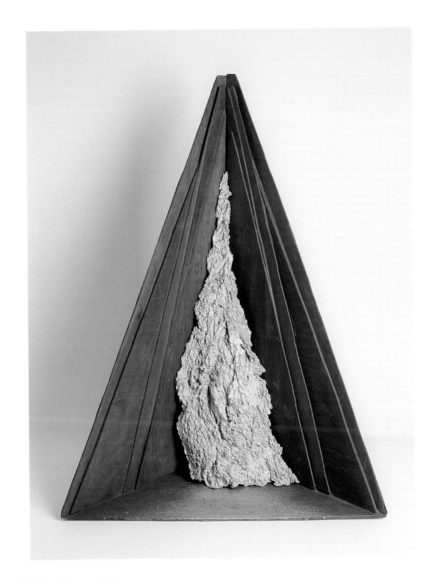

figure 47   Wide Valley 2002

Biography

1956-60
Slade School of Fine Art London,
Diploma in Fine Art

1971-72
University of Wales Swansea, Dip.
Special Education

1973-76
Open University, BA Psychology

1987-89
University of Wales Institute Cardiff, MA
Fine Art

Collections

Galleri Brinken, Stockholm, Sweden

Coleg Harlech, Harlech, UK

Vaughan College, Leicester, UK

Mid Glamorgan Education Authority, UK

New Hall, Cambridge, UK

and private collections in UK, Europe,
Canada & USA

Awards and Residencies

1990
Welsh Arts Council Masterclass

1992
Flying Hi. Sculptures for the County
Youth Dance Project

1993
Stackpole Centre Sight Garden,
Pembroke, Wales

1994
Visiting Artist, Homes for the Elderly,
Cardiff

1994
Leighton Studios Artists Residency, Banff
Center for the Arts, Canada

1994-1998
Arts Council of Wales Residency,
Groundwork Bridgend, Wales

2000
Greenfield Valley Meadow Mill
Millennium Sculpture, Flint, Wales

2001
Textile Residency, Raglan Primary
School, Wales

2002
Silent Valley Nature Reserve Residency,
Cwm, Ebbw Vale, Wales

Solo and Shared Exhibitions

1960   Galleri Brinken, Stockholm

1967   Llantarnam Grange, Cwmbran, South Wales

1968   Bristol Arts Centre, Bristol

1971   Vaughan College, Leicester

1974   Chapter Arts Centre, Cardiff
                (up to and including this exhibition Jackson was still using her ex husband's surname)

1989   *UWIC MA Degree Show:* The Old Library Gallery, Cardiff

1991   Malpas Library, Newport, Gwent
                Forms of Containment: Prema Arts Centre, Uley, Gloucester
                Three Artists: Prema Arts Centre, Bristol

1992   Central Library, Barry, South Wales
                Llandough Hospital, Llandough, Cardiff

1994   3rd Wave Gallery, Cardiff (this is the gallery which used to exist above Jacobs Market building)

1995   *Rock and Water:* St David's Hall, Cardiff
                (this was a large show of work from her Canadian and South Wales residencies and her
                Australian and Middle East travels)

2001   *Rare:* Washington Gallery, Penarth, South Wales

2003   *Valley:* Oriel Y Bont, University of Glamorgan, Pontypridd, South Wales
                Dilys Jackson: Watercourse: New Hall, Cambridge
                (New Hall has the largest collection of women artists' work in the UK)

Group Exhibitions

1954-56   *Cambridge Drawing Society:* The Guildhall, Cambridge
Jackson was the youngest member, being still at school. One of the oldest members at the time and was Gwen Raverat.

1958   Slade School Students Exhibition, Keble College, Oxford

1959   Exhibition of students work, Royal College of Art, London

1960   Queenswood Gallery, London
Young Contemporaries: London
The work exhibited was *Wendover in the Snow.* Jackson made several visits to the great escarpment and war memorial at Wendover.

1969   *South Wales Group:* National Museum of Wales, Cardiff
Jackson sold her first exhibited wood carving at this show, *Owl.* It was bought by Dame Irene White for Coleg Harlech.

1975   *Pictures for Welsh Schools:* National Museum of Wales, Cardiff
Arts Fayre: Chapter Arts Centre, Cardiff

1984   *Young Cardiff Artists (Association of Artists and Designers in Wales):* Turner House, Wales

1986   *South Glamorgan Women's Arts Festival:* Cardiff
This was the first of the annual festivals organised by members of the Arts Discussion Group of the Women's Committee of South Glamorgan. The Group later formulated itself into The Women's Arts Association, sometimes also called Permanent Waves.

1987   *South Glamorgan Women's Arts Festival:* Cardiff

1988   *All Women Work 88:* Chapter Arts Centre, Cardiff
All Women Work was a group formed from meetings and discussions at the first Women's Art Festival in South Glamorgan. The exhibition in Chapter had an arrangement of sitting room furniture at one side of the gallery where viewers could come in and relax. It was an attempt to take out the mystic and distancing of the gallery space.
Relic: Collective Gallery, Edinburgh
Sculpture for Gardens: Criccieth Festival, Gwynedd, Wales
Mid Wales Open: Aberystwyth, Wales

1988   *Cardiff Visual Arts Festival:* Cardiff
This was an event organised by members of AADW. It ran for a number of years and took place in venues all over Cardiff, such as empty shop fronts and Bute Park.
South Glamorgan Women's Arts Festival: Cardiff

1989   *All Women Work and the Magdalena Project:* SAAC Studios, Cardiff
The Magdalena Project is a women's theatre which works internationally, with the
continuous input of performers from all over the world. It has its base and its beginnings in Cardiff.
The visual artists work hung in the performance space, a huge black room. Jackson's work was
an installation of a 6x3m drawing of Harpies above netting and postcard images of the
Magdalene and Mary Magdalene, the performance theme.
Lower Machen Festival: St Michael's Parish Church, Mid Glamorgan
During the Music Festival at the church, artworks were sited in the churchyard. Jackson had two
works; Anti War Memorial and Proclamation.
Pictures for Schools Exhibition: National Museum of Wales, Cardiff
South Glamorgan Womens Arts Festival: Cardiff

1990   *Environment Friendly:* Phoenix Arts Centre, Leicester and tour
South Glamorgan Women's Arts Festival: Cardiff
Save St Davids': St Davids Dyfed and tour
This was an exhibition in aid of the clean-up of a huge oil spill.

53

1991   *Festival Exhibition 91:* Collective Gallery, Edinburgh
Postcard Show: Collective Gallery, Edinburgh
Works on Paper: Collective Gallery, Edinburgh and tour to the Commonwealth of
Independent States
This was a drawing from television images of the destruction of Baghdad during the Gulf War.
Jackson was a member of the Collective gallery in Edinburgh for a number of years.

1992   *South Glamorgan Women's Arts Festival:* Cardiff
Summer Show: West Wales Arts Centre, Fishguard.
Jackson became a gallery artist for many decades and sold a number of works from this gallery.
Impressive Women: London Print Workshop

1993   *Permanent Waves Arts Festival:* Old Library Gallery, Cardiff
Association of Visual Artists in Wales: Swansea
The National Eisteddfod of Wales: Powys
The Wales Open: Aberystwyth, Wales

1993   *West Wales Arts Centre Summer Exhibition:* Fishguard, Wales
Wales Arts Fair: Old Library Gallery, Cardiff

1994   *Permanent Waves Arts Festival:* Old Library Gallery, Cardiff, Wales
Wales Arts Fair: Old Library Gallery, Cardiff
Wales Open: Aberystwyth, Wales

1995 *Permanent Waves Arts Festival:* Old Library Gallery, Cardiff, Wales
Wales Arts Fair: Old Library Gallery, Cardiff, Wales
Blackmill to Bwlch: Nantymoel & Bridgend, Wales

1996 *Off the Wall:* Circle Gallery, Pontypridd, Wales
Permanent Waves Arts Festival Open: Central Library, Cardiff, Wales
Four Artists: Oriel Contemporary Art, London
ArtsFest Open Exhibition: Fishguard, Wales
Llantarnam Grange, Cwmbran, Wales
Harlech Biennale: Harlech, Wales
The White Room Gallery, Harlech, Wales
At this same time Jackson also had work in a virtual gallery on the internet called Iterating Spaces which was showing at the Biennale.

1997 *Arts Council of Wales Artists in Residence in South East Wales 1994-1996:* St David's Hall, Cardiff, Wales

Permanent Waves Arts Festival Open: St David's Hall, Cardiff, Wales
Artists Gardens: Washington Gallery, Penarth, Wales
The Countryside Exhibition: Gallery 27, Cork St, London
Off the Wall: Mold Museum and Gallery, Mold, Wales
Yr Adwy, The Gateway: Coed Hills, St.Hilary, Wales
Art with Groundwork: Bridgend, Wales
Art Auction in aid of the Tower Colliery workers, Cardiff, Wales
The colliery was threatened with closure. The workers bought the colliery which is still working.

1998 *Wall Works:* Cowbridge Old Hall, Wales
Womens Arts Festival Open: Washington Gallery, Wales.
Whitechapel Open: Carpenters Road Studios, London
For several years Jackson shared an Acme studio here with Imogen Ward.
Artists Against Arms: Cardiff, Edinburgh & London
This exhibition was in aid of the Red Cross.
Artists for the Environment: Civic Offices & the National Eisteddfod of Wales, Bridgend, South Wales
Jackson curated this exhibition of work by seventeen artists whom she had brought in to work on Groundwork Bridgend projects.

1999	*Beyond Nature:* Washington Gallery, Penarth, Wales
	Permanent Waves Arts Festival Open: St Davids Hall, Cardiff, Wales
	Quarry Landscapes-Sharing Visions: The Cowcross Gallery, London.
	Landscape and Arts Network organised this exhibition of responses to Tout Quarry in Portland. It was designed to support The Portland Sculpture Trust who manage this ancient quarry where artists can work.
	Its only paper: Stroud House Gallery, Stroud
	Christmas Show: Washington Gallery, Wales
2000	*Millennium Waves, Womens Arts Festival:* Craft in the Bay, Cardiff, Wales
	Inner Visions: Newport Museum and Gallery and Kingshill House, Dursley, Gloucester
	Terra Incognita - Images of Australia: University of Wales, Aberystwyth and tour
	Creative Connections: Bridgend, Wales
2001	*Visible:* St Davids Hall, Cardiff, Wales.
	Welsh Artist of the Year: St Davids Hall, Cardiff, Wales
	Ways of Seeing. Llanover Hall, Cardiff, Wales
2002	*Butetown Artists:* Bay Art Gallery, Cardiff, Wales
	Visible 2: Llantarnam Grange Arts Centre, Cwmbran, Wales
	Little and Large: Welsh Group, Museum and Theatre, Brecon, Wales.
	Celtic Exchanges: Sculpture Cymru and Sculpteurs Breton, Landisiau, Brittany and Barcelona, Spain
	Colour and Form: Café Verdi, Mumbles, Wales
	Celtic Exchanges: Pontardawe Arts Centre, Wales and tour.
2003	*Parameters:* The Welsh Group, Taliesin Arts Centre, University of Wales Swansea and tour
	Gross Innovations: The Welsh Group, Beverly Arts Centre, Chicago, USA

Publications

Learning From Art. Times Educational Supplement 1971

A Video Unit in Schools - Is it Worthwhile? British Journal of Special Education, Vol. 1, no 11977

The Women Artists Diary 1990. The Women's Press, London

Harpies and Quines. Front cover illustration, issue no 3 Oct/Nov 1992, A Collective Publication, Glasgow, Scotland

Beyond the Boundaries. Women in the Arts Project of the Arts Council of Great Britain and the Women's Caucus for Art (USA) 1993

Chasing the Dragon. Creative Community Responses to the Crisis in the S. Wales Coalfield. Chap: The Environment, p 57, 1996

Halech Biennale. Exhibition catalogue 1996

Yr Adwy/The Gateway. Exhibition catalogue, 1997

The Time of Our Lives - Valleys Autobiography 2. Chap.5 Illustration of the Terrace Houses Bench, Nantymoel. Valley and Vale. 1997

Dictionnary of British Artists 1945-1999

Terra Incognita - Images of Australia. Exhibition Catalogue, 2000

Butetown Artists. Exhibition Catalogue, 2002

List of Works

All photographs by Patricia Aithie except where stated.

Cover
REMWAS
(Ready Made War Scenarios) 1989
Wood and paint
240 x 450 x 1,800 cms

Photograph
Portrait with Jackdaw 1994
Photographer Deborah Doherty

Photographs
Studio portrait 1991 page 9
Studio portrait 2002 page 56

Figure 1
Life Painting 1959
Oil on board
129 x 91 cms

Figure 2
Wendover in the Snow 1960
Oil on board
91 x 22 cms

Figure 3
Indian Pitta 1945
Coloured pencil on paper
190 x 250 cms

Figure 4
Puppy 1955
Terracotta
9 x 19 x 11 cms

Figure 5
Owl 1972
Marble
40 x 40 x 20 cms

Figure 6
Lost Scrolls 1972
Wood collage on wood
123 x 144 cms

Figure 7
Dark Hanging Group 1974
Leather on wood
126 x 153 cms

Figure 8
Threatening Bird 1987
Mixed media on board
23 x 92 cms

Figure 9
Bodycase 1 1990
Wood collage
594 x 841 cms

Figure 10
Bodycase 2 1990
Acrylic monoprint & wax crayon
59.4 x 84 cms

Figure 11
Standing Stones 1988
Mixed media on board
144 x 104 cms

Figure 12
Derelict War Memorial 1986
Mixed media on board
122 x 91 cms

Figure 13
Victim Kuwait 1990
Monoprint, pastel & acrylic on paper
59.4 x 84 cms

Figure 14
Burning Cities 1989
Pastel on paper
59.4 x 84 cms

Figure 15
Balance 1 1991
Bronze
23 x 23 x 32 cms

Figure 16
Opposing Forms 1990
Aluminium
120 x 180 x 240 cms

Figure 17
Bronze 5 1991
Bronze
18 x 18 x 16 cms

Figure 18
Arch Formation 1995
Bronze
30 x 30 x 23 cms

Figure 19
Flow from Arch 1996
Bronze
24 x 16 x 18 cms

Figure 20
Bronze 1 1991
Bronze
38 x 30 x 15 cms

Figure 21
Sulphur Mountain 1994
Bronze, glass & wire
15 x 23 x 3 cms

Figure 34
Fire 1999
Bronze
21 x 16 x 16 cms

Figure 35
Blown Moss 1998
Bronze
16 x 8 x 16 cms

Figure 36
Quarry and Culvert 1997
Pastel on paper
74 x 55 cms

Figure 37
Long Stream 1996
Bronze
86 x 17 x 15 cms (wall mounted)

Figure 38
Rain Pool 1993-5
Stainless steel, brick & slate
10 x 500 cms

Figure 39
Waterworn 201
Portland stone
30 x 30 x 20 cms

Figure 40
Waterfall 2000
Stone and bronze
32 x 22 x 18 cms

Figure 41
Gorse 2000
Pastel on folded paper
15 x 13 cms

Figure 42
Head of the Valley, Spring 2000
Pastel on folded paper
15 x 13 cms

Figure 43
Forest Edge 2000
Pastel on folded paper
15 x 13 cms

Figure 44
Dark Valley 2000
Pastel on folded paper
42 x 28 cms

Figure 45
Rust 1999
Pastel on folded paper
59.4 x 84 cms

Figure 46
Garw Quarry 2002
Paint on moulded paper pulp
38 x 33 cms

Figure 47
Wide Valley 2002
Wood and bronze
82 x 53 x 27 cm

Acknowledgements

This record of some of my work, and at times, the production of my work itself, has been made possible through the support and encouragement of many people; of my family, friends and colleagues. In the case of this publication in particular I am glad of the opportunity to express my thanks to Dianne and Terry Setch for their steadfast friendship, their wise professional advice and their timely support as colleagues. I should also like to express my thanks to Julie Morgan for her commitment to the project which has sustained myself and many other women artists over many decades, to Patricia and Charles Aithie for their dedication to perfection, to Shelagh Hourahane for her skill in weaving word patterns from the many threads of my life and practice, to Ken Shaw of Groundwork Bridgend and Neath Port Talbot for his understanding of the time requirements of my work outside those of the Trust, to Martin Bellwood of MB Fine Art Foundry who casts my bronze works and to my sister Dinah Jackson for her meticulous work in checking the text.

Dilys Jackson 2003

61

Terry Setch

Terry Setch was born in Lewisham, London in 1936 and studied painting on undergraduate and post graduate courses at the Slade School of Art, University College, London. He has exhibited in major galleries in Europe, Australia and the British Isles.

Terry Setch has paintings in the collections of the Tate Gallery, London, The Arts Council of Great Britain, the Contemporary Arts Societies of Great Britain and Wales, the National Museum of Wales, the Victoria and Albert Museum, London and numerous other museums, local authorities and University collections in Britain.

Patricia and Charles Aithie

Patricia and Charles Aithie are photographers who specialise in photographing travel and the arts. They supply images to national and international book publishers, magazines and newspapers. Regularly working for artists, art organisations and publishers they document sculpture, painting, ceramics and the crafts in many books, catalogues, brochures and leaflets. Their own location work has taken them around the world photographing traditional culture and indigenous crafts. They have a wide experience of working in the Middle and Far East.

Dianne Setch

In 1985 Dianne Setch formed a Women's Arts Discussion Group for the South Glamorgan County Council which evolved into Permanent Waves Women's Arts Association, an organisation aiming to address the problem of women artists working in isolation.

In the late 1980s Dianne Setch developed an interest in digital arts after a varied career as an artist working as a teacher, a gallery exhibitions organiser and an arts administrator. A decade later she helped establish a digital arts workshop and has since managed the workshop which enables women artists to promote themselves using the new technology.

Shelagh Hourahane

Shelagh Hourahane is a free-lance writer, researcher, artist and lecturer. Born in Cardiff, she was for many years a full-time lecturer in Art History at the University of Wales, Aberystwyth.

She has been active as an exhibition researcher and writer on contemporary art in Wales since the late 1960s. She has written widely including articles on public art in Wales, individual contemporary artists and the landscape. The latter topic has become the main focus of her writing and recent art work. In the 1980s she was largely responsible for the foundation of the Welsh Sculpture Trust now know as Cywaith Cymru.Artworks Wales. In 2001, with Lynne Denman, she established Creu-ad, an artist group which works on community and interpretive projects in rural Wales.

Julie Morgan MP

Julie Morgan has been Labour MP for Cardiff North since 1997. She is a member of the Welsh Affairs Select Committee and chairs the All Party Group for Children in Wales and also the All Party Parliamentary Sex Equality Group. She is an executive member of the Welsh Labour MP's Group, the Labour Women MP's Group and also the All Party Human Rights Group. She is also Chair of the Cardiff & Vale Domestic Violence Forum.

Before becoming an MP she was a councillor in Cardiff and Chaired the Equal Opportunities Committee for South Glamorgan Council. She was a member of the Welsh Refugee Council and was Chair of the Albany Road School Governing Body.

Julie Morgan is a social worker by profession and worked in Cardiff and Swansea Social Services Department. Her last job before her election was as Assistant Director of Barnardo's in Wales, where she worked with children and young people.

64

Price £9.95
ISBN 0-9544439-0-X

9 780954 443900